LANGUAGE THAT ALL CAN SPEAK

A CHILDREN'S BOOK ABOUT KINDNESS AND DIVERSITY

This Olivka Book belongs to

....

To my cute, fun and stubborn Olivia! You are a whole world! Make it a beautiful one!
With all my Endless Love, Mommy

Language That We All Can Speak
A Children's Book About Kindness & Diversity
#1 Olivka Books

Olivka Books Publishing
www.OlivkaBooks.com
First Printing, 2020
ISBN: 979-8690873431

DEAR PARENTS AND EDUCATORS,

If you are holding this little book, you probably agree that we all need more kindness and acceptance in our hearts today more than ever. And the best time to learn it for our kids is now, while they are still kids.

This sweet and short story will show your kids the importance of being kind, will teach them to be more aware of other people's feelings, accept differences, and understand the beauty of diversity in our world.

After reading this book, try to engage with your kids by discussing some of the questions below. It will help better understand why diversity is beautiful and why it is essential to be kind to others.

Please do not force the process, only ask questions that your kids will understand. Be curious, kind, and patient with their answers. See if your kids have some questions of their own. Follow their interest and curiosity, help them understand this vital topic.

Some questions to discuss:
- Do you think kindness helps us to connect with other people?
- Each of us is precious, unique, and a little different. How are you different from your friends? How are you the same?
- What do you think word diversity means?
- What is most beautiful about your friends? What is most beautiful about you?
- Do you think that differences make our world beautiful? In nature, in animals, in people?

Download a Free Coloring Page to accompany this book at www.OlivkaBooks.com
Happy reading!

Warmly,
K Read

Olivka and her family were brand new in town.

They unpacked their boxes and got settled down.

Olivka sat and wondered, "Will I find new friends?

What kind of kids will be at school when summertime ends?"

Finally, school was starting and Olivka felt so great!
She'd meet new friends, play new games—she just couldn't wait!
She skipped off to school with a smile on her face.
Excited to find out if school was a fun place!

When the school was in sight Mom hugged her goodbye.

As Olivka rushed to the door, someone caught her eye:

A little girl with dark skin, a deep, silky brown,

Waved her and enthused, "Welcome to our town!"

In Olivka's home country most people were white,
Different skin tones and features were rarely in sight.
There they shared the same colors for skin, hair, and eyes.
Seeing kids look so different was quite a surprise!

The two girls walked to class, new friends, side-by-side.

They stopped at the door, where Olivka peeked inside,

Can you guess what she could see? All kinds of faces!

There were white and black and brown kids from different places!

There were big boys and small boys and all types of girls.
They had short hair and long hair, and some heads had curls.
There was black hair and blond hair and browns in-between,
And the shiniest red locks that she'd ever seen.

With a closer look, Olivka saw the eyes of blue.
She saw brown eyes, hazel, and eyes of green too.
She saw different noses—some cute as can be,
And the prettiest freckles she ever did see!

Soon she'd meet her new classmates—and how would that go?
Would they tease her or like her? She just didn't know.
How would they greet her? What would they say and do?
Olivka hoped that they'd all be kind and welcoming too.

She watched as a wheelchair rolled right past her feet,
"Excuse me," said Margaret, who sat in the seat,
"Are you new to our school? Would you like to play?"
Right away, Olivka knew—it'd be a great day!

At circle time, they sat, their legs crossed on the ground,
But one boy could not sit still—he jumped all around.
Their teacher, Ms. Lee, said kindly, "This is Trey.
He has some special needs. He learns his own way."

Then the whole class sang a song to learn each new friend's name
Every name was different—not one was the same!
Olivka's turn came and a thought crossed her mind.
Would they giggle at her name or would they be kind?

"Let's all welcome Olivka, she's new to our school."
Then a boy named Manu said, "Olivka? That's so cool!"
Manu had an accent; her name sounded brand new.
She liked his voice and his words, so she said, "Thank you."

At snack time Olivka's apple fell onto the floor.

Marcus shared his snack and said, "That's what friends are for."

He was generous and kind—that's just how he was.

He would share with every friend, simply because!

Next, Olivka built with blocks, way up to the sky!
But her tower wobbled and fell, needed one more try.
Danny, who had autism, didn't speak at all,
But he helped build it again—this time, twice as tall!

At art time, kids painted. Look! Red, yellow, and blue!

Every painting was special, and wonderful, too!

They mixed colors into orange and green, purple and gray,

And a million shades of brown. Fun with colors—YAY!

After a day of learning, and all kinds of fun,

It was time to go home now. The school day was done.

On the way home from school, Mom had a surprise.

"It's a beautiful secret, so please close your eyes."

Mom showed her a big garden, Olivka needed a pinch.
She was happy and surprised. She loved every inch!
There were nice red flowers, deep purple, and blue.
She saw little pink petals and yellow ones too!

And one whiff of those petals, the smell was so sweet,
Like fresh fruit or honey or some other treat.
Each flower was different—so unique and cool,
They reminded Olivka of her new friends at school!

We have our differences, altogether though
We make the world more beautiful than it's been before.

Each of us is precious, each of us is unique,
But kindness is a language that we all can speak.

Thank you so much for purchasing our first book!

We hope you and your kids enjoyed reading it as much as we enjoyed creating it! Please let us know if you have any feedback! We would love your input on making our next book even better.

Reviews are vital for small self-publishers like we are, and they truly help new books to be seen by more people. So if you have a minute, we kindly ask you to share your honest opinion about this book by reviewing us on amazon. Thank you so very much for your support!

More Olivka Books are coming soon. If you'd like to stay in touch and be the first to read them, please visit OlivkaBooks.com.

Warmly,
K Read